Shoveling Snow in a Snowstorm

poems by

John Jeffire

Finishing Line Press
Georgetown, Kentucky

Shoveling Snow in a Snowstorm

Copyright © 2016 by John Jeffire
ISBN 978-1-63534-063-1 First Edition
All rights reserved under International and Pan-American Copyright Conventions.
No part of this book may be reproduced in any manner whatsoever without written permission from the publisher, except in the case of brief quotations embodied in critical articles and reviews.

ACKNOWLEDGMENTS

The author wishes to thank the editors of the following sources for publishing these poems: *the detroiter* ("Shoveling Snow In a Snowstorm"); *Midwestern Gothic* ("Birth Certificate" and "Angel of Detroit"); *North Chicago Review* ("Man Swimming Off Belle Isle Swept Away by Current"); *Paddlefish* ("Detroit" and "The Horse and the Nail"); *In the Company of Writers Anthology* ("Hop In"); Uncommon Core ("Hesed"): *Oakland County 115* ("What We Talk About When We Talk About Love"); *Life Preserved Anthology* ("An Abandoned Motel, Gratiot Avenue"); *Epigraph* ("Psychiatric Ward, NYU Hospital"); *Gap-Toothed Madness* ("Stray Cat" and "The Stray Dogs of Sochi"); *Right Hand Pointing* ("If That's the Best You Can Do").

Publisher: Leah Maines

Editor: Christen Kincaid

Cover Art: Konnie Jeffire

Author Photo: Konnie Jeffire

Cover Design: John Jeffire

Printed in the USA on acid-free paper.
Order online: www.finishinglinepress.com
also available on amazon.com

Author inquiries and mail orders:
Finishing Line Press
P. O. Box 1626
Georgetown, Kentucky 40324
U. S. A.

Table of Contents

"Shoveling Snow in a Snowstorm" 1

"Birth Certificate" 2

"Psychiatric Ward, NYU Hospital" 4

"The Horse and the Nail" 5

"What We Talk About When We Talk About Love" 6

"An Abandoned Motel, Gratiot Avenue" 8

"Detroit" 9

"Catechism" 10

"What the Junkie Hears" 11

"Home From Eloise" 13

"Angel of Detroit" 19

"Man Swimming on Belle Isle Swept Away by Current" 20

"Hop In" 22

"The Stray Dogs of Sochi" 23

"The Nickel of Truth" 24

"Hesed" 25

"Coming Home, Detroit, 2015" 27

"Saudade" 30

"If That's the Best You Can Do" 31

"The Last Jew of Vinnitsa" 32

"Monarch" 34

Shoveling Snow in a Snowstorm

Bulimic Michigan winter belches
Gusting bowels of whiteout fury,
Green Ford pick-up engulfed
Beneath blind waves of ice,
Neighbors' homes capsized
In a squalling January tempest.
Wife marooned at work,
Kids swept away to college,
I abandon ship through the front
Door portal, wind tidalwaving
Into the foyer, intruder shouldering
Into the house, until I find myself
Cast adrift in the driveway
Clinging to a rusted shovel.
Cheekskin freeze-dried in air,
Fingertips vaporized in thermal glove—
There is absolutely no point
To what I am about to do.
It'll make it easier when the snow
Finally does stop someone who looks like me
Says inside my brain, the stupidest idea I've
Tried to convince myself of in months.
A snowmobile sails by in the street
And a mitten waves joyously.
I've shoveled snow my whole life
And where has it gotten me?
More snow always falls.
Shovels break, back muscles give,
Seas of breath lost in a flurry of grief.
I awaken to the sound of aluminum
Scraping along frozen cement.
The sky is an ocean of whirling stars.
It's snowing out. And me? I shovel snow.

Birth Certificate

At exactly 6:25 a.m. on April 6th, 1962,
I sprung dumb from the viaduct gutter
Outside Detroit Mount Carmel Mercy Hospital
Backed up with rainbows of transmission fluid,
Sogged defeated leaves, frayed tire treads,
And a dead Doberman's decayed bald paw.
I was the 121st birth that day, one of 874,
All of us sharing Mickey Cochrane's birthday
Just two months before he unstrapped his shinguards
And headed to the great dug-out in the sky.
E.W. Prichette, M.D., attendant at birth, confirms
I flushed full-formed from the East End's
Rectum, nickel pitching penis packing Athena
With a stew-pot helmet, singing
The fight song of an ivy walled college
That would never accept me on
Its most deluded day. That morning I bit
My own umbilical and spit the shank
Of flesh tethering me to the assembly-
Line of blank bank statements of
An overdrafted confession booth
And cracked a tooth. On April 19th, 1962,
C.P. Anderson, M.D., officially registered
The birth on account I had not come to
My two-week old senses and cashed out
Of the madness early, instead opting to
Let life play out in its choking monotony,
Flunked science tests, cheating girlfriends,
Flat tires and empty gas tanks, a stay in the
County lock-up, bosses who cared less that
I was alive let alone born than the ex-wife
And my cable rep. All this was certified in 1988
By the Honorable Coleman A. Young, Mayor,
On behalf of the Detroit Department of Health.

So I now present this document, the official
Confirmation of my every failure to be someone
Other than a seven pound, 11 ounce ghost crying
And shitting his way into the world, demanding
Fifteen minutes of love and respect, a paper
Stamped by the Great Maker and Governor
George Romney and Mayor Jerome Cavanaugh
And anyone else who would listen that
Johanna Marie Kuzemka (maiden name),
Born in Donora, Pennsylvania, and her
Husband Thomas W. Jeffire, Jr., of Detroit,
An apprentice at the Ford Motor Company
Who was too stewed at Bookie's Tavern
On Washington Boulevard at Grand River
To realize he had a second son scribbled onto
His ledger of mouths to feed, had bestowed
A gift of some sort on humanity, ammonia
Breathed, shrieking at the Packard Plant off I-94
My birth and this day were truly like no other.

Psychiatric Ward, NYU Hospital

The ward pay phone.
You pay and you pay and you pay
To use this phone.
You do it by the numbers now.
I need to speak to Lea.
White girl, blond hair.
The receiver is a scalpel
On a stainless tray.

The bone and tendons of her mind
Break in the steel jaws. You lie.
You tell her to sleep a pearly shell
Until you unspell reality, conjure
The horn-tailed monster called illness,
Find the weak plate protecting
The dragon's heart and strike.

One minute myth.
She must go.
Someone else needs the phone.

The Horse and the Nail

Every nail that finds a vein in your arm,
It's my heart turns to leather,
Unable to spit life into the next chamber.
The three-legged horse tripping inside you
Finds a girl at the bottom of a flight of stairs.

You can stop falling.
The floor gets no less dirty.
I surrender. Will you?

What We Talk About When We Talk About Love

Too many ways of looking
At a blackbird tossed
In the autumn sky.
From the dry shadows
Of the bed from which
The sun cannot step,
Your whisper flits above:
I am free to leave.
First, a living will,
Power of attorney,
No machines or tubes,
We first discussed this
When our hearts beat quick
In the raven's glimmer,
A clatter of wings burst
At red clay and live oak—
    Free to go.
The wind knows all directions.
I wipe feces from crevices
My tongue once explored,
I scrape uneaten meals
From cracked plates,
I dig arms under whatever
Is left to dig under—
So many ways of looking
At a blackbird thrown
In an autumn sky, life alit
In the few uncollapsed rivers
Of your hands, and I consider
The offer, freedom, mine from
You or yours from me not clear.
Stand with me, survey the distance:

Blanched earth, seedless,
Scab stubble frozen pools,
Creek frozen in its sheets,
The only proof of life its absence:
The bank gives way beneath our feet,
I grip the crest of your waist,
And one wing between us,
We take flight.

An Abandoned Motel, Gratiot Avenue

No pack of guests pocketing wedding bands
Named Mr. Smith paying cash by the hour could
Have saved this empty place, and they didn't.
Checkered salesmen from Peoria journeyed
To worship so quickly the sheets never
Needed changing, just a spritz of Lysol,
And escaped before daylight in sedans
Whose trunks were stuffed with samples
So stupid they actually worked. The false
Eyelashes rinsed in the sink with a washcloth
Frayed at the edges, patted dry everything
That had turned sour in life, beginning
With the modeling job that required
A screen test in another room of this
Very building. The concrete blocks that
Formed this concrete block of manic lust
And loneliness have a couple stories:
One about a salesmen slipped on a slick
February sidewalk and the insurance
Unpaid in years, then over-ripe Cherry
Found three days decayed in a bathtub
Ringed in rust, strangled with her own
Stockings, her lipstick smudged, and
   No last name on the register.

Detroit

I've quit counting the kicks
And yet battered dog that I am
I slink back, bruised, the past
Dried in salty pissing on my face.
I gave you a child's candy cloud
But you handed back a bloody ass
And a cancelled 3-cent postage stamp.
And every time you kicked my shit
And tripped my wire I found my knees
And crawled into your backseat.

You and your smug henchman god have
Washed my face in the manure of my days
And slit me scrotum to sternum and squeezed
My beating heart in your hands—and I stand.

Catechism

We sat as polished knobs,
our bobbing heads on springs,
performing our holy jobs
repeating sacred things.

When unruly eyes or wandering heads
strayed, Sister, armed with metal ruler,
rapped us from rapture until we bled
despite every covert ploy to fool her,

and yes, we wished her dead
with cancer and contaminated snot
despite all Jesus' words writ in red,
but a cuff on the head was all we got

and a workbook of lessons unlearned.
Yet we learned—to hate, to loathe—
which is exactly what we earned
years later, when we were all clothed

in divorce, jail, poverty, and shame.
Screw it. At least my knuckles healed.
Her words and threats were lame
as a jawboneless ass dead in a field

laid waste by grasshoppers and rot.
Hell, whether I want to admit it or not,
  We deserved exactly what we got.

What the Junkie Hears

Day two of a 10-day comedown,
In a briar brain burn you
Churn a soiled gurney,
Suboxone plodding veins,
Boring the bones
Of your hands and feet
Turned cold as winter stone.
Addiction whispers,
"Don't kill me."
A smile slits his
Meth trench face, his
Serpent teeth flicker.
"I was always there for you,
When the basement was empty,
The pipes thumped seduction.
In your name I sang you awake.
Please, please don't kill me."
His voice is a warm flood
Of euphoria jugular jabbed,
That much closer to the brain.
He's right. You love him.
"I'll make it up to you,"
He says, and his stained fingers
Caress your sweated cheek,
And you feel his tracked arms
Surround you in honey music.
"This time we'll get it right.
This time, the rush will never end."
And you believe as your marrow
Aches and heaves, your legs kick
At nothing without being told.
"This time, we'll do it right.
We'll know when to say when.
We'll leave this place,
We'll reshape your face,
Just one more taste, a taste."

He slips under limp covers.
As soon as you can stand,
You'll follow him to Lucifer's dumpster.
Who needs teeth, hair, a past.
You'll take the hit again,
Needle deep to the spinal chord.
Guts junkie rush your yellow mouth,
Tongue bloats a dead man's float.

Home from Eloise

I.
What made Millie say
It's better this way,
As the magician replaced
My socks with a gown
On that day I stopped
Counting the days?
I have one day now
And it retells itself
In a day without sun.
Time for exercise.
Walk the marshy ground.
There is no ground.
I float everywhere while
Cows stumble
The south fields.
Keepers never let us stray.
But I stray.
I still own a home on an avenue
And each day add receipts
For steel at River Rouge
That marches out disguised
As body parts for Henry Ford.
The road, over there,
The traffic dreams away
In honor of Mr. Ford,
Cars glint like toothy laughter
In the daylight,
But no roads lead here.
Escape, though, is everywhere.
A fall-out shelter in the dirt
For when the Russians
Keep their promise;
A lily floating on the man-made pond;

The viaduct under the rail line,
The Penn Central hooting to us
At night then churning to darkness;
The smokestack of the power house
That calls our ghosts;
The cemetery where we all become
A number carved on a brick.

II.
Keep that up
And we'll send you
To Eloise,
My mother jokes.
My brother and I
Are reliving the movie
Jason and the Argonauts
In the living room.
My brother is older
So he is Jason
And I am a legion
Of skeleton men
Who spring from
The snagged carpet.
From the couch
I leap and my brother
Cuts me down
And then from
A chair I vault
And again am destroyed.
My five year old bones
Have been breaking
Since a millennium
Before Christ woke
In Bethlehem,

And I leap and spring
And attack and fall.
Eloise, I think,
A riot of games
And make believe,
Endless cackling skeleton men
Brought down by a
Sword wielding hero.

III.
I apologized but
The woman at the desk
Smiled warmly and said,
You're not the first snowbird,
You won't be the last.
Later, Millie told me
I had been wandering
On the freeway without my coat
Or galoshes, that
I had wet myself at work
And drifted off without a word.
But how…gone, all of it gone.
She would never lie.
But why did she lie?
I knew where I had been.
I was at Belle Isle near
The aquarium on the grass
In summer, a picnic on a
Checkered cloth, my sons
Throwing a ball and laughing
On a breeze from the river.
I was perched on a wooden bleacher
In centerfield at Tiger Stadium
Lapping a Stroh's and passing
A piping redhot to a woman down the bench.

I was everywhere I had ever been happy.
And now I am here.
Again and again and again,
I am here.
Even the sewer grates remind me,
Eloise Hospital.

IV.
Don't open the door,
My mother warns
When Edna rings the bell.
Her voice is panic.
She's been in Eloise,
And that explains everything.
Edna is the same age
As my parents but
Her ravaged overcoat cloaks
Something we can't understand.
She lives three houses down
With her parents in a room
That's been hers since girlhood.
We hear her laughing
At night on our way home
From the baseball diamond.
Edna's eyes are penned leopards
At the Detroit Zoo.
She wants cigarettes.
Give her some damn cigarettes,
My father yells, and my mother
Looks at him before giving in,
Opening the door and quickly
Making her offering.
Edna is Eloise, and Eloise is not
A young fleshy cheeked girl and her dog
But a cigarette craving disease
We chase from our porch.

V.
The water tower is
An atomic bomb on stilts,
The smokestack our Babel.
We bake our own bread
And it is good, as good as
I've ever tasted.
Here, I work.
I brew coffee in the cafeteria,
Great bullets of hot life
That never run dry.
Pogie, I am called, having
Earned the title of
Poor Old Gentleman in Eloise.
I play cards in the smoking room
Of "N" building
And talk baseball and politics.
When Gordon curses Vietnam
I do not say a word about my brother:
Torn French countryside
Panzer diesel fuel rush
Foxholes and shelling—
A government letter of condolence
Two months late.
Mother said it was God's will
But loss is loss, and God's will
Is not my will and my will
Slips away like the hand
Of a young boy turned ash
Drifting from a smokestack.

VI.
I need to see Dr. Seymour,
I tell the young doctor
And he laughs, his face
As smooth and pure as snowfall,
Unmarked by the diagonal webs
Of grating covering every window.
We'll see what we can do,
He assures me, but he cannot find
A stable vein and blood
Seeps down my arm.
Medication heals the caring.
In "B" building, a grope and kiss
In a stairwell do not seem dirty.
I don't know anyone named Millie.
Someone said she left with Ed Thomas
And hasn't visited or written since.
Teddie, though, he visits in the night.
He asks if I've seen his ball and glove
And if he and his brother Steven
Can play an extra ten minutes
Before dinner.
Sure, son, play as much as you'd like.
I am a good father, a dependable husband,
A kind man, an honest employee.
But I have wandered off,
Become lost by the river, a
Snowbird with a ruined wing.
I now cry at nothing,
For no one and nothing and never again.
But please, if you can, answer me this:
If sadness is sickness,
Then who has not lived here
In this place?

Angel of Detroit

When you been done hard
by that bad thing
and you look up from
down a black hole
and the wind of bad luck
thick with misery
burn your eye black
as the river soot-swollen
ripe in bad blood—

the Angel of failure blessed
sit me on her mercy seat
and her offspring bring me
cool jars of jasmine wind
unblacked with riot smoke
and in that jade eye I am blind
to that bad thing and her black
promise of ash and earth

and that Angel open her soft hand
wide as they lion mouth
and you put that bad thing down
where the blacksnake smile
her midnight charm and lies
and the bad nickel shine
made new at that Angel lip—
the narrow gate wide open

Man Swimming Off Belle Isle Swept Away by Current

I mean, was he supposed to ask
Before he hit on the ex-wife?
A friend, yeah, but a poet, and
There's the rub. You tell yourself
That this is the kind of fucked up
Thing poets do, create dramas
In which they are the stars,
The emotional axis around
Whom all the rest of us are
Merely players awaiting our
Assigned marks and places.
And really, she's not my thing
Anymore, as if anyone is
Possessable, a "Property of…"
Tag stenciled to their chest.
And she had left me
Long before she left me, and
I was unfaithful long before
I was unfaithful.
I have no stones to throw
And need to let everything go.
Like finding out a friend
Has counseled my new woman
That she needs to date other men,
Confiding that she wished she
Had done the same before remarrying,
A marriage she professes to be
A happy and fulfilling one.
And I think "How the fuck dare you?
This woman has pledged her heart
To me and I to her and we've
Said things to each other
Under the holiest moon
Christened in each other's sweat,"

But regroup and say "Yeah, sure,
Why the fuck don't you?
You know nothing of nothing and
Nothing will change that."

So we end on a beach: a man
Trying to beat the late June heat
Gingerly tiptoes over broken
40-ounce bottles, syringes, pitbull
Shit and soiled diapers to the
Brown sand edging Belle Isle.
And he knows the Detroit River
Is not a river at all but a waterslide
Slingshotting all that enters it
From the ass of one massive lake
To the mouth of another.
But he also knows that at this head
Of beach Henry Ford has not
Yet begun to belch into the water,
And in reality his own sweat
Burning his eyes and his receding
Hairline and the wetsuit of fat trapping
The unbearable heat in him
Drawing him to seek water is
Really just a poet somewhere
Willing him to his mark or place.
The lung-snatching cool will
Feel so redeeming that he won't
Remember every poet he's ever read
And painted him betrayer and betrayee
And used and bullshitted him as he
Allows, yes, allows the current
To sweep him further from the shore,
Past Houdini's bridge, a flesh and blood
Wreck seagulls will peck at as it
Floats belly down past the Ambassador.

Hop In

At our age, we're all total carwrecks,
Samsonite blown off the trunk,
Soiled underwear and dryer burned shirts
Tumbling over the highway, loonies freed
From the asylum. Whose job it was
To tie the baggage down now moot
As the coffee stained map ten years
Out of date, charting a course on a stretch
Of two-lane road turned stripmall.
But there you are, lady, thumb up,
Cherry licorice stick legs and high beam
Smile hoping one more ride, safe passage
On a well-lit, smoothly paved freeway
To a gated community still on its hinges.
I'm not hiding my dented fenders,
Defective doorlocks and cracked windshield.
Coincidence, but I'm headed wherever
You're going, so hop in, buckle up, find
A favorite station on the radio, there's still
Gas in this tank and tread enough to burn.

The Stray Dogs of Sochi

This one scratches the fleas he picked up
In the cliffs surrounding Kabul. He answers
To the name Sasha, or Pasha, or Vladi
And he clearly remembers the fresh purple
Lotus bulbs burst from the fields pure
As that first hit from a comrade's pipe.
When the clouds of happiness no longer
Lifted the Taliban dagger dancing
Across his throat, he loaded the glass Scud
And sailed cosmonaut over the Volga.

Wandered west from the same bastard litter,
Keisha holds a markered cardboard collar
That reads, "Please feed my child."
Grenade haired, one unfocused eye
Hocking puss, her arms are tracked
From the foot of Mayor Cobo's Arena
To Herman Gardens, to a trap house
Two blocks off the Edsel Ford Freeway,
To an abandoned factory guarding
The Motor City Casino, to the slumping
William Livingston house at Brush Park,
Albert Kahn's purebred puppy hacking dust.
Here at a corner before Madison Avenue
Jogs onto 375, this stray begs bones
As a roach burrows into the darkness of
A cot at the Wayne County lock-up,
Hey, y'all hold that shit down, Lebron
James is explaining destiny on ESPN.

The Nickel of Truth

It doesn't buy much anymore,
But if you save enough of them
You can pay to replace the knees,
Aortic valves, disks, and dreams
You obliterated in their saving.
On one side, you've got shiny
Tom Jefferson looking off to Sally
Heming's quarters, hawking
Liberty and trust in god like
A plaid car salesman. On the
Flip side we covet Monticello,
Where he and Sally's mulatto
Children earned no last name,
No declarations or inheritance,
Just the right to be purchased in
Louisiana and a daddy too busy
Forging paper freedoms to
Come say hello in the fields.

Hesed

Before every leap
Appear several
Well-measured steps,
The kisses dreamed
Before the kiss.
So picture this:
A lifetime ago,
The crumpled old man
In the decaying frame
At the entrance
Is young and smooth;
As that young man,
He rolls his frayed sleeves
In the basement of
This very church
And shovels coal
Into a glowing furnace
Before winter sunrise
So the other worshippers
Have Sunday warmth.
Weeks turn years
And cross a century.
The coal dust
That settled into
The thumbs of his lungs
And squeezed the
Breath from him
And clung to his fingers
When he raised
The host to his lips
Meant nothing.
Yellowed photos
And fingernails and eye-whites
And a dying old man
Bleeding from his lungs
Are not this story,

But the black coal
Burning to whiteness
To warm those
Who would worship.

Coming Home, Detroit, 2015
 —for P.L., 2/15/2015

He had your back at Packard
And the Rouge, told the story
You didn't even know you owned
On the bootlegger's pier off Atwater.
He walked Chevy in the Hole
In Flint as it gagged alkaline into
The undrinkable fecal river.
The girls at Café Cablis so tired
They didn't notice the gropers
Too tired to grope, but when
He heard Long Eddie on the
Alto he lifted a filmy boomba
And passed the salt at the Polish
Village Café over a steaming plate
Of stuffed cabbage and pierogis.
Hell, he's the one who chucked
The brick at the Overpass that
Clipped old Harry Bennett and
Left the prick in stitches before
He handed Frankensteen a hankie
To sop up the blood streaming
Off Reuther's mashed up face.
Behind the counter at Detroit
Transmission, he made damn sure
That all those briefcases of capped
Teeth and their bleached high-ball
Wives beside the club pool didn't
Dare equate you with the cairn of
Bolts and sheet metal humping the
Pointless cadence of your days.
 But you didn't know. How could you?
You can't name the last book you
Ever touched and can't claim to
Have ever finished one in your life.
And he was straight with that because

He understood how you returned
The punched time card to its smudged
Slot, found your hat and wool jacket,
Thermos and tin dinner pail, and
Headed to the monthly debt
On wheels where you pushed
The coffee-browned want ads
Off the front seat onto congealed
Food wrappers and empty waxed cups
With crippled straws still trying
                    To stand upright.
And he understood because he, too,
Had slid the key in the ignition
And turned, igniting no ideas,
No epiphanies, no way around or out.
He knew both what work was
And what it sure as hell wasn't.
It was his hand caught in the lathe,
His fingers on the shop floor.
The oil and grime beneath your
Remaining nails was his, and it would
Only flee if you peeled those nails
Back with plyers and bit down hard,
And for a split second you think
That might actually feel good.
The radio says someone important
Has died so you change the station,
Unwilling to feel any worse over one
More thing you can't sand away.
You never met the man who rattled
The rag of your life on an upright
Wurlitzer missing half its keys, like
Rolling up the driveway to find
Some stranger has shoveled the
Walkway to the front steps where

Inside a woman awaits, brewing
You tea and fixing a ham sandwich,
The family dog near death at her heel.
And it's probably best that way.
You sit in the driveway a moment
For no reason, notice the way the
Moon defies darkness as daylight waits
Beyond the freeway to push them both
From the sky, flipping the headlights off,
Taking a good deep breath, performing
The daily sacred and silent ritual of
Sliding the transmission into park,
Reaching for the door latch, then
Stepping out into the burned air
To make your way inside.

Saudade

I started wearing your perfume
Last week after I ran out of
Aftershave, you know, your bottle
With the fancy flower shaped
Glass lid, I don't know the name,
And then I began wearing your pajamas,
The blue ones with the holes I should
Have replaced months ago. And I
Hope you're laughing as you
Read this, because of all my jobs—
Run to the grocery store at midnight
For mango ice cream guy,
I hate to say this because we're
Already in bed but I left my
Cellphone in the car guy, or honey,
The dog shit on the carpet guy—
My favorite job, the one I feel
I'm best at and enjoy most,
Is being your clown. I wasn't
Born a crusted set of pennies
Under the passenger side floor mat,
You just found me that way, camped
In a mattress on the living room carpet,
Two crates for a dining room table,
A blender, plenty of dog food, the
Frig empty except a twelve of IPA,
So what I mean, what I'm trying
To say in some small way, is *Lady,*
Come home, soon, please come home.

If That's the Best You Can Do

All breath begins in a desert,
Picking up sand and armies
And lifting them, scattering them
Where they will never be found.
Echoes replace what made them
And are replaced by cities, chrome,
And highways headed elsewhere.
This is where we choose: to be
Lifted from the earth and spat
Like a seed from the cannon mouth
Of a god, or to be lifted from
The earth and spat like a seed from
The cannon mouth of a god.

The Last Jew of Vinnitsa

Victory is hard work but Bingel
Says we are nearly finished
And we are all eager to be home.
I carried bag after bag of lime
To the edge of the pits
And it was greatly tiring.
With such victory, the war
Will be over very soon.
We are all ready for holiday.
It was rather funny that we told them
They were to report for a census
Near the airfield and then had them
Place their valuables on the tables.
Can you imagine their surprise?
It was great sporting fun.
I have secured a rather nice ring
And a few other such items for you.
I hope that you are pleased.
The airplane engines are very loud
And hurt my ears severely.
I have been eating well enough.
The sausage here is passable
        But it's not home.
The temperature is agreeable
And the locals are friendly enough.
Some of the natives have even
Been enlisted to assist in the process.
Vinnitsa and nearby Uman
Are pleasant enough
        But it's not home.
These people truly disgust me
And I am glad to be rid of such filth.
They took off all their clothes, even
The women, and showed no shame.

Toward the end we did not even
Bother to have them undress
And just finished our job as is.
I am most proud to be a member of
Einsatzgruppe D and the work we do.
They are a fine group of fellows
And most fun to share a beer with.
Can you believe the final count
Topped the 28,000 marker?
The leadership is very pleased with us.
Victory, though, is very hard work.
I am anxious to walk with you
Along the river and hear the sweet
Music of your voice.
The *Umanka* is a stream of swine piss
Compared to the Rhine.
The work is finally done.
Victory is hard work but
Bingel says we are nearly finished.
I've enclosed this picture
To show you what we do.
Imagine the nerve of this fellow.
Look, it is almost October.

Monarch
—for Olga Klekner

Butterfly, petrified death mask of
that morning frozen to tree bark
a day after being lifted weak and
fluttering from seedless dirt, milkweed
thirst pulsing in a failing heart.
He expired pure as he remains,
the veined fire of his stippled wings
aglow with eye whites, unscarred
by kingbird or orb weaver fang.
Up State Road, condemned scars,
tattoos, beards and braids washed
before a walnut throne, papal white
beneath blue chambray, the first last,
monarch frozen in supplication,
inclusion of excluded ending confinement,
still life of place without place in a place
where darkest debt is forgiven.

John Jeffire was born in Detroit. In 2005, his novel *Motown Burning* was named Grand Prize Winner in the Mount Arrowsmith Novel Competition and in 2007 it won a Gold Medal for Regional Fiction in the Independent Publishing Awards. Speaking of *Motown Burning*, former chair of the Pulitzer Jury Philip F. O'Connor said, "It works. I don't often say that, but it has a drive and integrity that gives it credible life....I find a novel with heart." In 2009, Andra Milacca included *Motown Burning* in her list of "Six Savory Novels Set in Detroit" along with works by Elmore Leonard, Joyce Carol Oates, and Jeffrey Eugenides. His first book of poetry, *Stone + Fist + Brick + Bone*, was nominated for a Michigan Notable Book Award in 2009. Former U.S. Poet Laureate Philip Levine called the book "a terrific one for our city." For more on Jeffire and his writing, visit *writeondetroit.com*.

Additional praise for *Shoveling Snow in a Snowstorm*

"John Jeffire's poems wrestle with life, and teem with muscular, inventive language. "But please, if you can, answer me this:/If sadness is sickness,/Then who has not lived here/In this place?" These poems are a fearsome ride which digs deeply at the surface of things, and leads us to shovel snow, sit in a psychiatric ward, to work in the River Rouge in Detroit, to look inside our hearts. These are works of survival, of praise for the way life and love can still surprise like a punch. "So what I mean, what I'm trying/To say in some small way, is Lady,/Come home, soon, please come home.""
—**Nadia Ibrashi**, winner of the X.J. Kennedy Prize

"There is fire in these poems, fire and ash and smoke, and the ghost of Phil Levine is kept alive by poets like John Jeffire who aren't afraid to honor such a debt. These are poems that know the city of Detroit and its history that they come from and remain faithfully tethered too. This is poetry that makes use of the world around us and reminds us what it means to be alive inside our own skins, which like a poem is its own kind of temporary song."
—**Peter Markus**, author of *The Singing Fish*

"From the crevices and corners of Detroit's post-industrial decay come John Jeffire's fierce and fiery poems. There's no respite from the brutality of cheap motels, psychiatric wards, abandoned factories or the lives lived around them, but the poems themselves stand in triumph—"a gift," as the poet writes of his birth, "of some sort to humanity." Tough, noir, proud, loving, refusing to mourn, Jeffire's poems capture the enduring voice of the working class and, like Philip Levine whose spirit he so ably invokes, spit in the eye of hypocrisy and oppression. It's exhilarating to read poems like these, poems that have nothing left to lose."
—**Terry Blackhawk**, Kresge Literary Fellow, 2013

www.ingramcontent.com/pod-product-compliance
Lightning Source LLC
LaVergne TN
LVHW041557070426
835507LV00011B/1136